Happy Birthday Elliot
Charlie

D0793001

LUMMIS
in the Pueblos

LUMMIS
in the Pueblos

by PATRICK T. HOULIHAN
and BETSY E. HOULIHAN

AN ENTRADA BOOK

NORTHLAND PRESS
FLAGSTAFF, ARIZONA

Front cover: The Silversmith
Frontispiece: Painter Albert Lujan of Taos
Back cover: Charles Lummis's shadow (foreground), bridge at San Felipe over the Rio Grande;
detail, p. 115

All photographs reproduced in this volume are the
property of the Southwest Museum, Los Angeles,
California, and may not be used without per-
mission.

Copyright © 1986
by Patrick T. and Betsy E. Houlihan
All Rights Reserved
First Edition
ISBN 0-87358-407-4 softcover
ISBN 0-87358-417-1 cloth
Library of Congress Catalog Card Number 86-60515

To Our Parents

CONTENTS

PREFACE

THE RESEARCH for this volume began in late 1981 soon after we moved from Albany to Los Angeles. Both of us were fascinated by Charles Fletcher Lummis and both of us recognized the historical and cultural importance of his photography. The decision to restrict our efforts to his Pueblo imagery was made in large part by our own longtime interest in the Pueblos. His other southwestern and California Indian photographs, as well as his camera work in Latin America, are just as valid and important, and we invite others to examine them for possible publication.

Throughout this project our efforts were fairly well defined. Betsy did almost all of the primary research and Patrick did most of the writing. Together we made selections of photographs and together we agreed on the general direction of the commentary. Concerning this commentary we tried to keep Lummis and the Pueblos the central characters and to maintain our text for both at the level of interest to a general reader and not that of a Pueblo or Lummis specialist.

Personally we feel enriched by the experience of researching and writing this book and we hope that a similar pleasure occurs for the reader.

ACKNOWLEDGMENTS

OF THE MANY PEOPLE to be acknowledged here we feel we must begin with our sons, Mark and Michael. Both endured too many weekend and prolonged evening absences to the work of this book. Also generous of their time and their home were Paul and Jean Dyck, at whose ranch in Rimrock, Arizona, much of the final manuscript was typed. At the Southwest Museum, the librarian, Daniela Moneta was especially helpful to us. Other staff members, including Stuart Ruth, Yolanda Galvan, and Cornelia Holt helped with the translations of Lummis's diary. A volunteer, Carolee Campbell, was of particular assistance in documenting Lummis's early photographic techniques. At the Los Angeles County Museum of Natural History, John DeLeon, made prints from the Lummis glass plate negatives. In Phoenix, we wish to thank Barton Wright for sharing so much of his knowledge of Pueblo Indian culture. Finally, we wish to thank Charles F. Lummis, whose vision created the Southwest Museum as well as the documentary record of Pueblo Indian culture presented here. In both the museum and his photography he left a priceless legacy for future generations to discover.

INTRODUCTION

OF ALL THE PHOTOGRAPHERS active in the American Southwest during the nineteenth and early twentieth centuries, few were as colorful as Charles Fletcher Lummis. Addressed by friend and foe alike as "Charlie," "Lum," or "Lummis," he was a slight man of enormous energy, which he poured into such causes as Indian and Hispanic civil rights; the preservation of the Spanish missions of California; the collection of Indian and Hispanic art, artifacts, folklore, and music; the establishment of the first museum in Los Angeles; and the general promotion of the West, which he termed "the left side of the Continent."

Although best remembered as a writer (of more than 450 books, monographs, articles, stories, poems, and translations of Spanish documents) and as an editor (of *The Land of Sunshine* and *Out West* magazines), Charles Lummis also left an important corpus of photography from his travels in California, the Southwest, Mexico, and South America. This important legacy only now is being rediscovered and exposed, largely as a result of the centennial events commemorating his walk from Ohio to Los Angeles in 1884-85. The goal of this publication is to examine that portion of the photography of Charles Fletcher Lummis that relates to the Pueblo Indians in the American Southwest.

The story of Lummis's "tramp across the continent" in 1884-85 is one that has been told and re-told in numerous publications. That we never tire of hearing it speaks to the appreciation we have of someone who responded so decisively to a compelling call to adventure. It was on this transcontinental walk that Lummis first encountered the Pueblos and commenced an association that would continue throughout his life.

Born in Lynn, Massachusetts, on March 1, 1859, Lummis was educated in the Classics at home by his father, a Methodist minister and educator. As a young boy he read Greek, Latin, and Hebrew. In 1878 he entered Harvard College, where, by his own admission, he majored in "Poker, Poetry and Athletics." Lummis left Cambridge in 1881 following his marriage to Dorothea Roads, a young woman studying medicine in Boston. He then went to live with and work for his father-in-law in Chillicothe, Ohio. There he managed a large farm for a year before accepting a position as editor with the *Scotia Gazette,* a local newspaper. By 1884, Lummis had arranged to sell copy, written as he traveled by foot from Ohio to Los Angeles, to the *Gazette* and the *Chillicothe Leader* and to Colonel Otis of the *Los Angeles Times.* His by-line during this trip was "Lum." It was this 140-day walk that Lummis recalled seven years later in his book *A Tramp Across the Continent,* based on his earlier stories of adventures and impressions of America.

Arriving in Los Angeles on February 1, 1885, Lummis went to work the next day as an editor for the *Los Angeles Times.* He stayed with the *Times* for three years (1885-88), after which he returned to New Mexico, where he lived at Isleta Pueblo until 1892. During these three years with the *Times,* Lummis learned photography. Also while employed by the *Los Angeles Times,* Lummis covered the Apache wars in southern Arizona. There, in 1886, he observed the Tombstone, Arizona, photographer Camillus Fly, who photographed the surrender of Geronimo to General Crook. He described Fly as "a nervy photographer from Tombstone, who had gone into Geronimo's fortress the day before, and 'took' the whole place and everyone in it." It seems likely that this experience with the Apaches and his observance of Fly may well have influenced Lummis to photograph the Pueblos.

As a photographer, Lummis worked primarily with two printing processes: the cyanotype and the salted-paper print. The cyanotype (from the Greek words meaning "dark blue impression") was invented in the early 1840s. Its use continues to the present day as the blueprint process, an inexpensive means for copying architectural plans and drawings. In the cyanotype process, photographic paper is coated with a mixture of ferric ammonium citrate and potassium ferricyanide. When exposed to light, the chemical reaction causes the paper to turn an insoluble shade of Prussian blue. Such paper is exposed beneath the glass plate negative, cleared by a water wash, and then dried.

The sun is the most effective light source for cyanotype printing because the chemicals utilized are particularly sensitive to the ultra-violet rays in sunlight. Such solar printing is generally done between 11:00 A.M. and 2:00 P.M. when the sun is strongest and most directly overhead. The length of exposure time as well as the intensity of the blue color will vary with the season. Many nineteenth-century photographers used the cyanotype print as a trial print, much the way modern-day photographers will use a Polaroid print. The cyanotype image is often referred to as the "sun print."

Lummis's isolation at Isleta Pueblo and elsewhere in the Southwest contributed to the contamination of his chemicals. There he rarely used distilled water or properly stored his materials. The results can be seen today on many of his prints where there are spots, stains, and a fading blue color.

In his unpublished autobiography, "As I Remember," he wrote of his photography in Isleta Pueblo:

> It was even harder to do my developing. But I made in this time many thousands of 5 × 8 plates, developed them and made my blue print. For silver prints I had to take my negatives to Albuquerque. If there is anything that is something of a test, it is to develop two 5 × 8 glass negatives at a time in an adobe room with a big basin bowl for a sink, no outlet except the outside door, no running water, nor other water except what was brought in *tinajas* (Indian pottery jars) and without any other facility whatsoever.
>
> I cut myself pretty badly several times where there were reef edges on the glass—for which my chief concern was that the blood spoiled the negatives. But of that host of pictures made at that time, while nearly all are interesting, there are very many that are unique and can never be made again—of types that are dead, buildings that are destroyed, ceremonials that are no more.

The cameras and lenses employed by Lummis are not all known. One of the earliest lenses he did use was a Dallmeyer. The Dallmeyer lenses were a standard and common outdoor lens for photographers of the nineteenth and early twentieth centuries. Dallmeyer produced the first rectilinear lens in 1866, which consisted of two achromatic lenses mounted in a tube with a diaphragm between the two lenses. The Dallmeyer lens reduced the distortions of earlier, simpler lenses. Thus, for example, rectangular objects or buildings could be photographed without the edges of the image seeming to bend. Its shutter speed was f.8. Lummis also used a Kodak in later years, but even at the end of his life, he continued to use his large box camera with the Dallmeyer lens.

We know from his diary and published writings that Lummis was using a Dallmeyer lens along with a Prosch shutter in 1888 when he first photographed in New Mexico. He would trip the shutter with a handheld bulb and count out the exposure time. His experience and luck sustained him. It is known also that he enjoyed the difficulty involved in packing his equipment when on foot or horseback. This physical exertion seemed to add importance and accomplishment to the otherwise simple act of tripping the camera shutter to capture an image.

It was while he was in New Mexico and living at Isleta that Lummis met Adolph Bandelier, the Swiss ethnologist and historian for whom Bandelier National Monument near Santa Fe is named. Bandelier exerted an important influence on Lummis and on his photography in the pueblos, not only by his companionship but also by his informal instruction of Lummis in Pueblo culture. Later, in 1892, Bandelier provided Lummis with the opportunity to travel and photograph in Peru and elsewhere in South America. The extent to which Bandelier directed Lummis's early photography is not known, but the former's scholarly influence had to be felt. Lummis also relied on Bandelier for expertise and scholarly authority for his writings.

In the Southwest, Lummis used his travels to gather photographs and information for his writing and thus earn a living, albeit a modest one. Lummis sold both written copy and photographic illustrations of the subjects treated in his writings, and undoubtedly this enhanced book sales for his publishers. Sometimes these photographs were themselves printed, and on other occasions artists employed by newspapers, magazines, and book publishers made illustrations based on his photographs.

Lummis was often in need of money to support himself and his family. To supplement the income he derived from his writing, Lummis also sold picture postcards and Indian "curios." In his later years, he drew on his inventory of images from both the Southwest and South America for the postcards.

The greatest source of primary information to be found on Charles Lummis comes from his diaries. They begin on February 5, 1888, when he left Los Angeles for New Mexico, and they end on November 12, 1928 just before his death on November 25, 1928. This self-record of forty years, as well as the scrapbooks he maintained of his published newspaper and magazine articles, are the sources for much of the research in this volume. Beyond these sources are his books, other articles and journals, as well as the

4

Charles F. Lummis in New Mexico, 1888

published works by others about the man. However, more than any other source, the diaries of Charles Fletcher Lummis place his movements in the pueblos with considerable certainty, and when combined with his photographs, they tell a story of Pueblo cultures in change.

The Spanish term *pueblo,* meaning "town," was first used by Spaniards in the New World to distinguish town-dwelling agriculturalists from other Indian groups. For example, elsewhere in the Southwest, the Pima and Papago Indian farmers of the Gila and Salt rivers in Arizona were referred to by the Spaniards as *rancheria* Indians, due to their residence pattern of isolated ranches or farmsteads stretching along a river course.

In 1540, when the Spaniards first arrived in New Mexico and later Arizona, approximately sixty pueblos existed. Today, as in Lummis's time, there are twenty-one Pueblo groups that belong to four major language families (Tanoan, Keresan, Zunian, and Hopi). For the Tanoan language family there are three important divisions: Tewa, Tiwa, and Towa. It should be noted that some of these Pueblo tribes, such as the Hopi, occupy more than one village. Lummis traveled to virtually all of the pueblos as well as to some Pueblo sites that had been abandoned in prehistoric or earlier historic times. Invariably, wherever he traveled he photographed. Unfortunately for some of the pueblos, he photographed only the Catholic mission church, or the dance plaza, or the kiva (an underground ceremonial chamber). Here we have limited our presentation to images of pueblos about which he wrote extensively; hence, not all of the existing pueblos are represented in this volume.

Beyond merely documenting the Pueblo people and culture by his photography and writing, Lummis fought for their rights. By his writings, lectures, and lobbying activities, he championed their concerns in education, land and mineral rights, and in historical and cultural preservation. Some of his language when read one hundred years later appears self-aggrandizing and insensitive. This was not the case, and his writing style must be read in the context of his time, keeping in mind that the subject of his writing was anything but popular.

Although our knowledge of the Pueblo Indians has expanded enormously since Lummis's travels, we are greatly indebted to the research of Lummis and his contemporaries as a base for later scholarship. Despite the fact that he was opinionated and wrote for general audiences, some of his observations are no less valid or important. However, his photographs more than his writings provide a priceless record of Pueblo culture. It is something of this record that we have sought to share.

ISLETA PUEBLO

THE TIWA-SPEAKING PUEBLO OF ISLETA, a dozen miles south of Albuquerque, was home for four years to Charles Fletcher Lummis. Beginning in July 1888 and ending in October 1892, Lummis lived at Isleta, and during these years he traveled by train, horse, and on foot to the other pueblos. After 1892, when Lummis moved back to Los Angeles, he returned to Isleta on numerous occasions, at least until 1906.

Making a home at Isleta was in part conditioned by events in his personal life. In 1888 he had left his first wife, Dorothea Roads Lummis, in Los Angeles and relocated initially at the home of his friend Amado Chavez of San Mateo, New Mexico. He had met Amado Chavez on his transcontinental walk in 1884. Four years later he was experiencing a partial paralysis of his left arm and side, generally thought to have been induced by the stress of both his job as an editor at the *Los Angeles Times* and by his deteriorating marriage to Dorothea. From his diary of 1888, it would appear that he established himself at Isleta in late July of that year. Recent scholarship by Ted Jojola, Ph.D., of Isleta Pueblo and the University of New Mexico, has shed considerable light on the circumstances that surrounded Lummis's entrance and acceptance by the people of Isleta.

Under Spanish and later Mexican rule, Isleta was the southern colonial headquarters of New Mexico. By 1850, Isleta was losing its position as the commercial and political center of the Rio Abajo, the "lower river." With the occupation of Santa Fe in 1846 by American forces, that city was designated the territorial capital, and the previous Spanish colonial civil administrative practices that had been continued under Mexican rule came to an end. Also by 1879, the Isleta right-of-way for the Santa Fe Railway had been negotiated, and with the railroad came an enormous increase in American influence on the pueblo. A significant part of this influence can be characterized as the conflict of a Protestant-American officialdom with a Catholic-Pueblo culture.

The two most direct circumstances bearing on Lummis's position in the pueblo were his own paralysis and the influence of the Abeita family, Lummis's landlord in Isleta. In 1883, five years before Lummis's arrival, the *cacique* at Isleta was paralyzed, and he remained in this condition until his death four years later. More than governor, a Pueblo *cacique* is a theocratic ruler who holds title for life by virtue of personal qualities as well as membership in prescribed religious groups and social organizations within the pueblo. Thus the appearance of a paralyzed Charles Lummis at Isleta one year afer the death of a paralyzed *cacique* was viewed in the pueblo as a coincidence of religious consequence. Concerning the Abeita family, Jojola states that in Lummis's time they "held a notable position in the general community."[*] Members of the family were proprietors of a store in the pueblo, owned and operated a horse-powered threshing machine, and in general were among the wealthier, more powerful families of Isleta.

The one-room house that Lummis rented from them was within the residence compound of the Abeita family. This compound was located on the fringe of the pueblo near the church and close to the most traveled road into the village. In effect the Abeita family sponsored and protected Lummis at Isleta.

While at Isleta, Lummis ended his marriage with Dorothea Roads. Following his divorce in February 1891, Lummis married Eva Francis Douglas, a young woman he had met at Isleta. Eve (or Eva) taught school at the pueblo and lived in the household of her married sister. Eve's brother-in-law, Archibald Rea, was a trader living in Isleta. When Eve was sixteen, she arrived at the pueblo to live with the Reas. In a few years she mastered both Spanish and Tiwa, then the two most important languages at Isleta. Her assistance to Lummis, both in terms of integrating him into the pueblo as well as his photography, cannot be overstated.

More than at any other pueblo, Lummis's photographs of Isleta capture the daily life activities of men and women. It is almost certain that he sought to document such activities, knowing that one day soon they would be lost. Since many of these tasks are performed by women, one could also assume that Eve's help with these photographs was essential. His portraits of Isletans are also numerous, as

---

*Unpublished paper read at the Southwest Museum, Los Angeles, February 1985

A view of Isleta, looking at the east 1899

are his images of houses and church architecture.

In article after article, Lummis described Pueblo culture, often in terms of a specific pueblo, but usually with a reference to Isleta. Hunting, games, religious rituals, folk tales, and social life all were detailed with references to his Isleta experiences. It seems fair to say that Lummis's view of the Pueblos was conditioned largely by his Isleta experience.

Lummis's contact with Isleta did not end with his and Eve's return to Los Angeles in October 1892. He made many return visits, and a constant stream of Isletans came to his home in Los Angeles. Some came to assist Lummis in building the house he called El Alisal, the Sycamore, along the Arroyo Seco in East Los Angeles. Other Isletans came as members of a dance troupe to perform at the annual Fiesta de Los Angeles. And still others came to work as house servants in the Lummis home.

In August 1906, tragedy befell an Isleta house-boy named Procopio. He was murdered at El Alisal by another of Lummis's house servants—a Spanish folk singer named Amate.

This death, along with the growing domestic discord between Eve and Lummis, brought an end to the employment of Isletans at El Alisal. More significantly, this tragedy caused an estrangement between Lummis and Isleta and perhaps with all things Pueblo. His diaries record no visits to Isleta from August 1906 until December 3, 1917. In addition to the death of Procopio, many Isletans objected to his publication of Tiwa folklore in 1894, in *The Man Who Married the Moon and Other Pueblo Folk Stories* and in 1910, *Pueblo Indian Folk Stories*.

As described by Jojola, today the memory of Lummis at Isleta Pueblo is mixed. Many still remember his efforts on behalf of the Pueblo through the Sequoia League, an Indian rights movement that Lummis championed, and still others remember him and his camera. Whatever these memories, Lummis's record of pueblo life at Isleta is unique.

Opposite: *A Corner in Isleta as seen from the northeast 1899*

10

12

The Cacique and his Wife and Daughter   1892

Opposite: *The Cacique, Pueblo of Isleta, N.M.   1892*

A Tigua Maiden   1896
As with Hopi women, the hairstyle indicates marital status. The Isleta tie the hair of
unmarried girls in a wrapped bun at the back of the head.

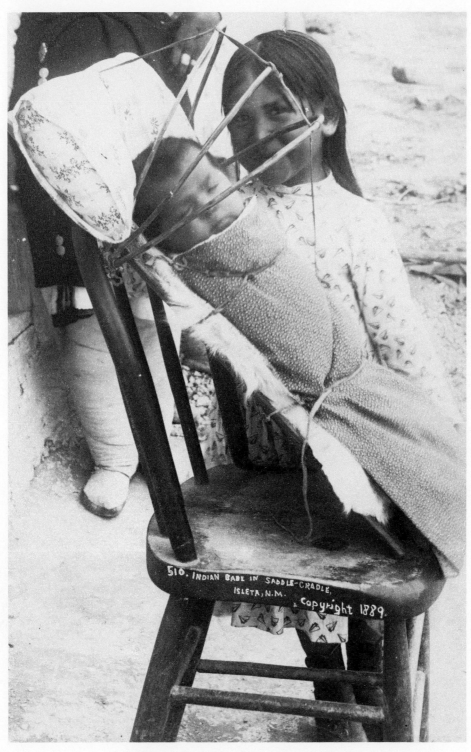

Indian babe in saddle cradle 1889
Two children from the family of Vicente Abeita

Ramon and Juan   1890
Note the condition of both boys' moccasins.

16

Children at the Acequia   n.d.
These irrigation canals provide countless hours of recreation for Pueblo children.

Viejo Chavez and Family   1900
The leggings he is wearing are made of goatskin and would be worn while farming.

Tiguas of Isleta   1895
The older spelling of Tiwa is Tiguas, and this latter spelling was often preferred by
Lummis.

Tata Lorenso   1889

Opposite: *Young Isleta girl in window   n.d.*

Blind Colas   1896
The use of a young child as a guide was quite common.

Tigua Sisters   1890
The setting for this photograph is used repeatedly by Lummis. The ladder, window,
and spotted adobe wall are all recognizable in a number of photographs. In all
likelihood this was within the compound of the Abeita family and close to his own
living quarters. Note that the same style of boot worn by the older sister is also worn
by the younger.

LUMMIS
PHOTO

41-INDIAN GIRL, PUEBLO OB ISLETA

Queres Mother and Daughters   n.d.
"Queres" is the earlier spelling of Keres or Keresan, and by using it, Lummis is
identifying one of the Laguna families who moved to Isleta after 1879 or 1880.
These Laguna migrants were religious conservatives who fled Laguna and were
welcomed at Isleta. The mother's costume, with the possible absence of a square cloth
tied about her neck and draped over her shoulder, is identical to that worn by the
Tiwa-speaking women of Isleta.

Opposite: *Indian Girl, Pueblo of Isleta   n.d.*
Seen behind this girl are corn, melons, and chilies that are being dried and readied for
storage indoors. The kitchen utensils and crockery in her hand are non-Indian, and
in striking contrast to the rest of the scene.

25

Side of the Church at Isleta   1900
The heavy buttresses seen here function to support the walls and roof. Their beehive
shapes belie the fact that they consist of adobe bricks whose rectangular shape is
hidden by an outer layer of mounded plaster. The wood bell towers on either side of
the front facade as well as the center cross were added in the 1870s.

Opposite: Church Interior, Isleta Pueblo   1899

Pueblo of Isleta, N.M., Feast of the Dead   n.d.
On the feast of All Souls', November 2, the women of the pueblo bring candles and
bowls of food to the unmarked graves of relatives who are buried in the cemetery
courtyard of the church. Lummis first described Isleta's Day of the Dead rituals in an
article by that title in the San Francisco Chronicle, *January 6, 1889. Note that*
only the women are in the graveyard on this day; men are seated on the wall or
perched atop the church.

A Pueblo Footrace   1896
The spring footraces in Isleta. Note the headband and costume differences of the
runners.

A view of the Isleta spring footraces   1896

Pueblo Indian kitchen fireplace   1890
Opposite the hearth in the right rear corner of this room is a doorway leading to a
living and sleeping room. The hood above the hearth would catch and confine smoke
and heat. This may be a room in Lummis's house at Isleta. Note the covered water jar
to the left of the hearth area.

Pueblo Woman Making Guayaves   n.d.
Guayaves are a wafer-thin "bread" made from corn flour. Among the Hopi it is
called piki. *Here a woman prepares it on a large pumice-stone griddle by spreading*
the flour-paste thinly across the stone with her fingers. The fire beneath the stone
quickly bakes it. After removing it from the stone, she has placed each guayave on a
stack beside her.

Pueblo Woman Sweeping Before the Fireplace   *1889*
Such short-handled brooms were made of bundled twigs or grasses. In some pueblos
they are bound in the middle and either end is used, depending on the purpose.

Pueblo Woman Weaving Belt   1894
The loom this woman is using is most commonly referred to as a back-strap loom. It
is secured at one end to a peg in the floor, and the weaver maintains the warp tension
by leaning back against a waist strap that holds the other end of the loom. In back of
her feet rests one of the loom's heddles. The blanket on the bed is probably Pueblo. On
the wall are Spanish santos.

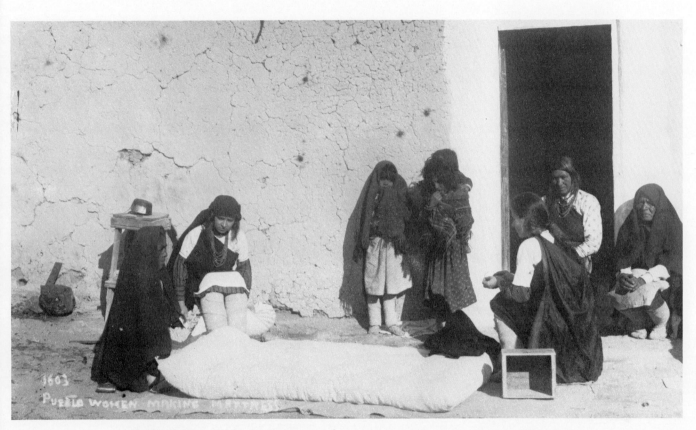

Pueblo Women making mattress   n.d.
Here a group of women and young girls watch as one of them stuffs a mattress with
wheat straw.

An Aboriginal Toilet   1890
This scene is of a woman brushing a man's hair in preparation for binding it. The figure in the rear as well as the central male both wear woven garters on their legs below their knees.

562. PUEBLO INDIANS PLAYING PATOL.
COPYRIGHT 1890.

Pueblo Indians Playing Patol   1890
This native game of chance was described by Lummis in numerous articles. It consists of forty round stones arranged in a circle, with four openings between every tenth and eleventh stone. A large cobble is placed in the center, and against it are dropped three marked patol sticks. How they land, i.e., what designs are shown, determines the movement of a player's marker or "horse" around the circle. The competition may involve two or more players and can last for hours. One of Lummis's descriptions of the game appears in the magazine Harper's Young People, *November 4, 1890.*

Opening the Main Acequia   1894
Here we see an early spring activity—men working on the irrigation canal,
preparing it for use in the coming growing season.

Indians Opening the Acequia   1894
This is a close-up view of the above photograph. This spring activity is an occasion of
communal work by the pueblo's males. Two canals, north and south of the village,
brought irrigation water from the Rio Grande to the pueblo's fields; cleaning and
maintaining these canals were the responsibility of adult males.

Threshing Machine   1890
This horse-powered threshing machine was used to process wheat and possibly to bale
the wheat straw. This machine was probably owned by the Abeita family.

Pueblos Winnowing Wheat   1891
Here wheat is separated from its chaff by walking on it and then tossing it into the air
with long-handled forks. The wind separates and carries off the chaff while the
heavier wheat grains fall to a canvas or textile placed on the ground. The corral-like
structure keeps the animals away from the wheat.

Winnowing   1890
Here a Pima Indian basket from Arizona is used to winnow, or wind-separate, the chaff or other inedible parts of the bean plant that may have been harvested inadvertently. The basket is held high in order to catch the wind.

A Pueblo Pottery-making 1890

A young woman is firing pottery vessels beneath slabs of animal manure in the center of her fire while drying other pots of different shapes and sizes on the perimeter of her fire. She is using an open fire that allows air to circulate over and under the vessels. In front and in back of the fire she has stacked more manure slabs, which are also used as her source of fuel. With the long pole she is able to reposition either the pottery or the fuel.

42

Tourist pottery from Isleta   n.d.
This pottery was probably made for sale to tourists at the railroad station nearby or
to one of the Indian traders in the pueblo. Most of these forms are not traditional but
reflect the commercial tastes of tourists at the turn of the century.

Baking bread in a beehive oven   1890
Just as the house wall in back of it, this oven is constructed of adobe bricks that are
then covered with adobe plaster. Wood is first burned to heat the oven, then removed
and replaced with the dough to be baked into bread. A small wooden paddle used to
place, position, and retrieve the bread is used here to hold a piece of metal across the
opening while the bread is baking. Such ovens were introduced by the Spaniards and
the Spanish term horno *is used to identify them.*

Opposite: *Isleta man with lasso   1890*
A lasso such as this would be made of a long piece of twisted rawhide, probably from
the hide of a steer or horse.

-1135-
A PUEBLO
WINE-MAKING.
COPYRIGHT 1891 BY
C.F.LUMMIS

46

A Pueblo Wine-making   n.d.
Grapes as well as wine-making were introduced to the Rio Grande Pueblos by
Spaniards. The movement of the people resulted in an unclear image.

Building a home at Isleta   1900
The men seen here are laying adobe blocks to form the walls of a pueblo house. The previously made adobes are stored on edge. The wet mud-mortar is seen as a darker color in the half-finished wall. To the far right, almost out of the photograph, are the roof beams, and next to the beehive oven are the latias, *or lattice sticks, that are placed between the beams. Above these beams and lattice sticks will be a layer of mud plaster that will serve as a roof.*

Pueblo Women 'Encalando'   n.d.
Each year a fresh coating of mud plaster must be applied to the adobe walls. This prevents rain, snow, and other moisture from reaching the adobe bricks and causing them to deteriorate. This mud plaster is applied by hand and is generally the task of women.

48

A Pueblo Silversmith   1900
At the turn of the century, Pueblo silversmiths worked silver by melting and casting the molten silver in sandstone molds. They also fashioned silver jewelry by wroughting, i.e., by alternately heating and hammering it. Note the small hand bellows in the foreground used to intensify the heat from a small fire, and the anvil made from a section of railroad rail.

LAGUNA

BETWEEN 1888 AND 1913, Lummis visited the Keresan pueblo of Laguna on twenty-three different occasions. In all, he was there for approximately thirty-six days. During four of these visits (1888, 1889, 1890, and 1901) he timed his travel to the pueblo in order to attend the feast of San Jose, which he photographed in 1901. Today, approximately two dozen Lummis photographs of Laguna have survived. It should be noted that of the six villages that are home to Laguna people, only the village of "Old Laguna" was photographed by Lummis.

That Laguna was a special place for Lummis is probably explained by a visit he made there, riding on horseback from Isleta in June 1891. The occasion was his honeymoon trip with his new bride and second wife, Eve Douglas Lummis. It was a trip of more than fifty miles, and his journal for June 20, 1891 reads:

> Eve and I started horseback on our belated honeymoon trip and rode 50 miles from Isleta to Laguna bogging down in the Rio Puerco, and the last 8 miles with Eve in my saddle, I holding her on. It's a long ride for a woman and she insisted on her fine sidesaddle. She never rode it again.

Also of importance to Lummis was the use of at least two of his Laguna photographs as the basis for paintings by the artist Henry Farny of Cincinnati, Ohio. Although best known as a painter of Plains Indians, Farny used Lummis's photograph of the interior of the pueblo's mission church as well as his long distance view of the pueblo itself as the subjects for two paintings. These paintings were published in *Harper's Magazine* of February 1891 in an article titled "The Heart of the Desert" by Charles Dudley Warner.

Laguna Pueblo   1890

51

Pueblo of Laguna, An Alley to the Plaza 1890

The dress this Queres woman is wearing is a single large piece of woolen fabric woven by a male. Such a textile is generally black and is referred to by the Spanish term manta. At the top and the bottom of the garment, a weaving change occurs in the pattern, such as a twill weave. The shawl she wears is Mexican. n.d.

536. PUEBLO MOTHER D GHT
COPYRIGHT 18

Pueblo Mother and Daughters 1890
In all likelihood, the pot on the young girl's head is from Zuni Pueblo. The walls of
this adobe house are in need of replastering; the window, only partially visible, is
Anglo.

54

Opposite: *These three young girls are washing wheat in the San Jose River*
adjacent to Laguna Pueblo.   n.d.

57. PUEBLO LAGUNA, N.M.

The mission church at Laguna Pueblo was built early in the eighteenth century. n.d.

The interior of the mission church of San Jose de Garcia at the Laguna Pueblo   ca. 1890.
The painted designs on the wall were originally red, yellow, and black. The symbolism most apparent is that of birds, rain, and clouds. The paintings on the main altar are attributed to an unknown Mexican provincial artist today called "the Laguna santero."   n.d.

This photograph was made in 1901 during the celebration of the feast of San Jose. The mounted spectators are Navajos who have ridden into the pueblo to watch the rituals. n.d.

A close view of the Navajo spectators seen in the photograph on page 58.   n.d.

This cart, or carreta, *is based on a Spanish model and was probably made without nails. Such carts would be hauled by a horse, mule, donkey, or ox.   n.d.*

ACOMA PUEBLO

THE KERESAN-SPEAKING PUEBLO OF ACOMA is often cited as the oldest inhabited town in the United States. When first visited by Spaniards in 1540, it had been in existence for more than six hundred years. It is generally thought that the sun's reflection on the pueblo's translucent mica windows caused the Spaniards to think they were made of precious metal—gold or silver. Such was not the case, for the Acomans were simple agriculturalists concerned with maintaining their traditional lifeways. To this end, they resisted Spanish attempts to subjugate them in 1598 and participated in the Pueblo Revolt of 1680 by killing their resident Spanish priest.

Between 1888 and 1913, Lummis made sixteen trips to Acoma. His diaries suggest that he was there for approximately forty-five days. He also visited and photographed at the nearby Acoman villages of Acomita and McCartys, but the vast majority of his photographs are of Acoma village itself as well as the ancestral site of Katzimo, the Enchanted Mesa. It was the controversy over Katzimo (or Katzima) that brought Lummis and Acoma Pueblo a great deal of notoriety in the years 1897 and 1898.

During his first trip with a camera to Acoma in 1888 (June 23, 24, and 25), Lummis made a series of photographs that relate to the festivities that surround the Feast of San Juan. These were reported in an article he wrote for the *San Francisco Chronicle* (July 29, 1888) entitled "A Pueblo Feast, St John's Day in Airy Acoma." To give *Chronicle* readers a sense of being there, he wrote:

When the first gray sky in the east turned to opal on Sunday morning all Acoma was awake. Warmer grew the shifting tints and at last the blood-red disk floated above the stunted piñons of the eastern valley wall. Upon the tops of their high terraced houses the children stood motionless and reverent; swathed in gorgeous blankets, bedecked with lavish silver and coral, their buckskin calzones bound with generous amplitude of brilliant garter, their long, soft hair restrained in silken kerchiefs or queued behind in Egyptian pigtails, their fine figures statuesque as a Grecian marble, their keen eyes full upon that blinding orb in whose beneficent powers they may well be pardoned for worshiping divinity. Five minutes later the motionless groups had broken up. From a hundred tall adobe chimneys, crowned with inverted earthen pots, the sleepy morning smoke curled skyward. Here and there a rainbow-blanketed form glided noiselessly along the solid rock of the lop-sided streets, and out by the great rock cistern beyond the noble church might be seen coming the stately line of maids and matrons marching homeward, each with a bright-hued tinaja full of water poised gracefully upon her shawled head, while below her quaint high boots of white buckskin shimmered in the level sun. . . .

Although not as important an occasion as the feast of St. Steven or the harvest feast, St. John's feast day is noted for its *gallo* (rooster) race or procession. In his article on Acoma, Lummis describes this procession, the earlier activities in the pueblo's church, and the running races of the Acoma men. Even in Lummis's time, he notes the large number of visitors (including Acomans from McCartys and Acomita) to the old village on the mesa top. Today, the majority of Acomans live below the mesa and use the old village atop the mesa as a kind of shrine-center for public ritual activities.

Although he took no photographs at the time, Lummis first made contact with Acoma during his walking "tramp across the continent" in 1884-85. He reported back to Ohio via letter the origin tale of Acoma, which the *Chillicothe Leader* published on December 12, 1885, and which he published again in the January 1890 issue of *St. Nicholas Magazine*. By Lummis's informants' account, the original home of the Acomans was the nearby Katzimo, or Enchanted Mesa, which stood out more than four hundred feet above the surrounding plain. To reach the summit, its inhabitants scaled several scores of steps hewn into the rock itself. However, the first two hundred feet were reached by steps carved into a massive boulder leaning against the mesa.

Legend had it that tragedy struck Katzimo one summer when all of its inhabitants, save for three old women who were sick, went to the plain below to prepare fields and to plant crops. A summer wind and rainstorm swept aside the banks of sand and rock that stabilized this huge stepped-boulder. As a consequence of this storm, the boulder rolled away from the mesa, leaving the three old women stranded and immediately causing the surviving Acomans to seek a new village site. The three women died, one by leaping to her death, and in time a new village was built atop another mesa a few miles away. Such was the legend in brief that Lummis first reported in 1885.

It was this obscure Pueblo legend that later propelled Lummis and Acoma to national attention. In July 1897, Professor William Libbey of Princeton University and two journalist companions, H. L. Bridgeman of Brooklyn and Mr. G. M. Pearce of Albuquerque, surmounted the Enchanted Mesa by means of a ship's lifeline fired from a mortar. After the lightweight line was passed over the mesa, successively larger ropes were hauled over the mesa by teams of horses. Using ropes and a bosun's chair, Libbey's party scaled Katzimo. After spending approximately six hours unsuccessfully searching the mesa top for signs of earlier habitation, Libbey and his companions made their descent. They promptly labeled the earlier Lummis story a hoax and renamed Katzimo "The Disenchanted Mesa." Lummis, of course, was humbled, but not totally defeated. He publicly questioned Professor Libbey's expertise in archaeology and continued to defend the importance of oral traditions as a legitimate source of historical evidence about the American Indian.

The American press, from Boston to San Francisco, covered the controversy, and Lummis filled a large scrapbook with articles about it. In time he was able to write editorial comments in longhand above and beside each Libbey installment.

Lummis was vindicated in September 1897 when F. W. Hodge of the Smithsonian Institution, along with Major George H. Pradt, a government surveyor at Laguna; Mr. A. C. Vroman, a photographer from Pasadena, California; Mr. H. C. Hoyt; and two Pueblo Indians succeeded in scaling the Enchanted Mesa. The Hodge Party found potsherds, broken stone axes, fragments of a shell bracelet, and a stone arrow point. In addition, in the talus slope formed by debris swept down from the mesa top by wind and rain, they found abundant evidence of prehistoric occupancy on Enchanted Mesa.

On September 5, 1897, Hodge sent the following note to Lummis from Laguna, New Mexico:

My dear Mr. Lummis:
I have just returned from Mesa Encantada where, with Major

Pradt of this place, A. C. Vroman of Pasadena and a Mr. Hoyt of Chicago, I ascended to the summit on the afternoon of the 3rd. The "Princeton (N.J.) Press" for August 21 which contains Libbey's report—all about those prehistoric flocks of sheep, Montezuma & the rest of the common rot that only a clean cut ass could write . . . & came down the following day about noon. We found good evidence of former occupation, on that you will hear something from me a little later—also Libbey. If you can, send for a copy of [text not legible on original] will send you photos later.

Sincerely yours,
F. W. Hodge

Lummis had his day in the October 1897 issue of *The Land of Sunshine* in his article "The Disenchanted Libbey" and again in the November 1897 issue with the article "Katzimo the Enchanted" by Frederick Webb Hodge. The latter article contained a number of the Vroman photographs taken on the mesa.

The following June, Lummis climbed Katzimo along with David Starr Jordan, president of Stanford University, and a party of Stanford faculty, students, and their wives. During the trip, Lummis again photographed the Enchanted Mesa as well as Acoma itself. It was obviously a moment of triumph for Lummis.

Pueblo of Acoma—East Side—Mesa Encantada in distance   1891
The free-standing mesa just to the side of Old Acoma is Katzimo, the ancestral home
of the Acomans.

A view of Acoma framed by the balcony of the convento   *1898*

Within the Pueblo   n.d.
To the left above the man leading a horse, a woman is weaving and another is hanging clothing on a pole. The plastered house wall is made of mortared stone, not adobe bricks.

Pueblo of Acoma, N.M., The Gateway   n.d.
This scene occurs on the pathway leading to Old Acoma.

Pueblo of Acoma, N.M., The Reservoir   n.d.
This reservoir has been used by many American painters as a backdrop; unfortu-
nately, some artists have placed Pueblo figures in non-Acoma costumes in the scene.

Katzimo 1898
The Enchanted Mesa, or Katzimo, rises 430 feet above the surrounding plain and is
located about three miles northeast of Acoma. By tradition, Katzimo was one of the
ancestral homes of the Acomans. This legend was first reported by Lummis in 1885
and again in 1890. Later, the legend thrust him into a press controversy when it was
challenged in 1897 by Professor William Libbey of Princeton University. Libbey
scaled Katzimo and declared it absent of any earlier human habitation. Lummis was
vindicated by a subsequent archaeological survey of Katzimo by F. W. Hodge of the
Smithsonian Institution.

Opposite: *Camino del Padre, Acoma 1898*
This boulder-strewn incline is a footpath leading to Acoma. The small seated figure
is Lummis's daughter, Turbese; the identity of the standing figure is unknown.

Indian Trading Post   n.d.
One of the owners of this post was Solomon Bibo, the first licensed trader at Acoma
(1882). Bibo was married to an Acoma woman, and his business dealings at Acoma
in the nineteenth century were the subject of much controversy. Lummis first
encountered the Bibos in 1884 during his "tramp across the continent." Bibo and his
wife were the subject of at least one dispatch to the Chillicothe Leader *and the* Los
Angeles Times *in 1885.*

Acomita   n.d.
Acomita is located about fifteen miles north of Acoma Pueblo. Originally a summer village used only during farming season, it gained an increasingly larger year-round population with the coming of the Santa Fe Pacific Railroad to northern New Mexico in the late nineteenth century.

The Silversmith, Pueblo of Acoma, N.M.   1891
This man is titled in Lummis's scrapbook as "Juan Lujan or 'Musico', chief silversmith of Acoma."

Opposite: *Lorenzo Lino, Governor of Acoma 1901*

LORENSO LINO, GOV. OF ACOMA. 1891
LUMMIS

Pueblo of Acoma, N.M., The Old Governor   1890
In his scrapbook, beneath a copy of this man's picture, Lummis identifies him in
Keresan as "Kai-A-Tan-Ish" and in English as "Martin Valle, Seven times
Governor of Acoma."

Queres Father and son, Acoma   1891
Lummis identified the man, Jose Concho, using the older spelling of Keres; the
language of Acoma is Keresan.

Washte Garcia, the oldest of the Queres   1891
In an article on the Katzimo controversy for the San Francisco Chronicle
*(September 26, 1897), Lummis identifies this man as one of his "authorities for the
legend of the Enchanted Mesa."*

Opposite: *Pueblo Farmer Irrigating Wheat   1902*
Lummis identifies this man as "Faustino, War-Captain of Acoma."

80

The Church and convento at Acoma   n.d.
The walled courtyard in front of the church serves as a graveyard for the pueblo.
None of the burials here will be marked. This area in front of a Pueblo church is thus
hallowed ground.

Opposite: *Interior of Church, Acoma   n.d.*

Following pages: *Dance of San Estevan   September 2, 1892*
San Estevan (St. Steven), the first martyr of the Catholic Church, is the patron saint
of Acoma. His feast day is celebrated on September 2 with a large fiesta at Old
Acoma. During the day, the saint's image is removed from the church, marched
about the pueblo, and then placed in a temporary shelter in the dance plaza. During
the dance, groups of men and women from different kivas dance separately. The
women dancers are clearly identified by the tablita *headpieces. The dance lasts all*
afternoon.

632—PUEBLO OF ACOMA
DANCE OF SAN
ESTEBAN
COPYRIGHT 1892 BY
C.F. LUMMIS

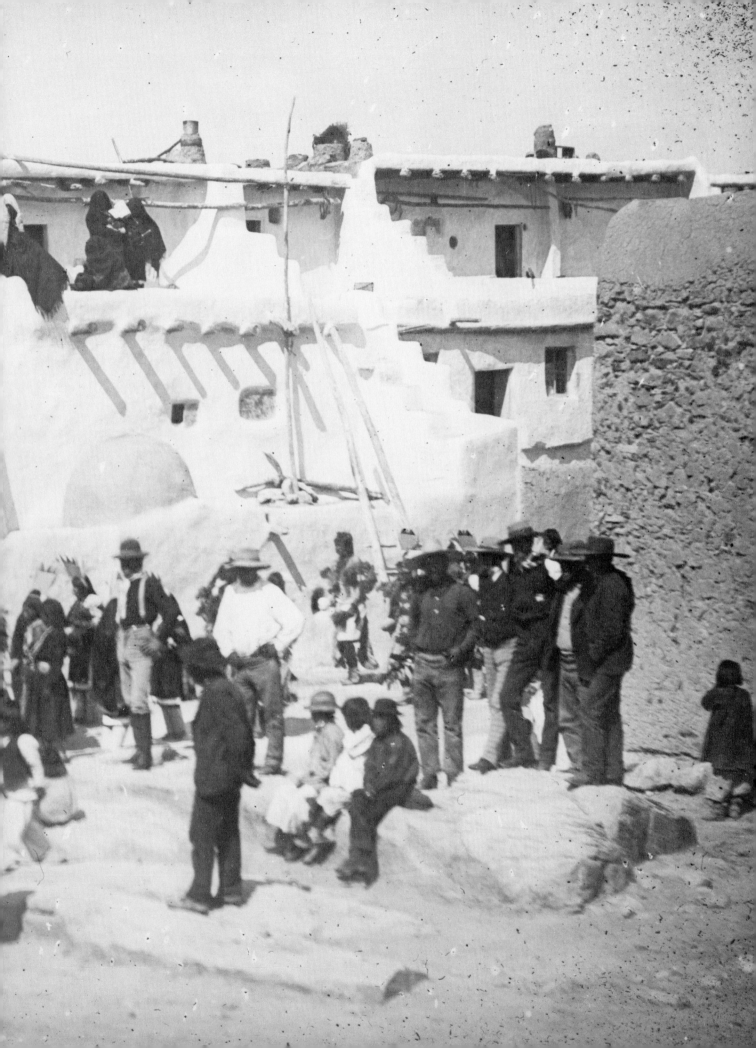

San Juan's Day, Acoma   July 6, 1898
Although difficult to distinguish, the figures descending the slope are mounted men
in a horse race.

Opposite: *Pueblo of Acoma, N.M., Procession of San Estevan   September 2, 1889*
The image of St. Steven is being carried on a litter from the church to a shelter in the dance
plaza.

ZUNI

ZUNI IS THE COMMON NAME of the Pueblo tribe located in northwestern New Mexico. In their own language they refer to themselves as *Ashiwi,* and to the early Spanish explorers of the sixteenth century, the Zuni were believed to be residents of the fabled Seven Cities of Cibola. In fact, the seven towns that Coronado encountered in 1540 were a group of villages not unlike the pueblos on the Rio Grande. However, the Zuni language is unique, for it has no known linguistic affiliation with any of the other pueblos of the Southwest.

Today approximately five thousand Zuni live in and around a single large village on the banks of the Zuni River. However, at the time of Lummis's visit in the late 1880s, its population is estimated to have been about fifteen hundred.

Lummis visited Zuni once for three days in April of 1889 and used the experiences and knowledge he gained from this single visit to write the article "A Day in Zuni" for *Drake's Magazine* of August 8, 1890. In this article, Lummis describes his arrival beginning at the small train stop:

> We had come down from Manuelito the day before, with much tribulation and a buckboard. Johnny Mason's mule was also implicated in the invasion. By the way, if you should ever wish to visit Zuni, stop at Manuelito, the last station in New Mexico going west on the Atlantic & Pacific Railroad, and subsidize Johnny Mason, the tall young freighter, to drive you to the pueblo, thirty miles south. But don't—oh, don't—let Johnny take his mule. Wait until he can find his horses, if it takes a week. For to the mule depends a tale—that is, in

addition to his own legitimate appendix. But let us not dwell on that now.

Concerning Zuni in relation to the other pueblos, Lummis had these remarks:

> With the exception of the Moqui villages, Zuni is the least visited of all the score of pueblos, and is consequently one of the most interesting. The railroad ruins an Indian with marvelous rapidity, and even these quiet Children of the Sun, who are not Indians at all, but true Aztecs, "Grow no better fast" under its baleful influence. Therefore if you would visit the aborigine, find him as far as possible from all the adjuncts of that dubious thing which calls itself civilization.

It should be noted that Lummis's understanding of Pueblo culture increased greatly over the years. Thus his early references about "sun worship" and the like are generally absent in his later writings. His notes on taking photographs at Zuni are even more descriptive:

> It is bald, unredeemed aggravation to visit a Pueblo town without a camera, and I was fully armed with a 5 x 8 box, and a Porsch shutter. But in these places one should have an outfit invisible, self-focusing, and qualified to take a picture in the millionth part of a second. The Pueblos share the Navajoe superstition about photographs, and my appearance around a corner with camera in hand was the signal for an instant and incontinent stampede of the whole visible population. Children flew, women ran, and the most dignified old men "got"—in the classic diction of the West—"an immediated move on them." We had to be content with photographing what buildings we wished, and then masking our battery in some obscure corner, taking a focus down street and waiting for victims to straggle along. In this bush-whacking fashion we secured some very valuable instantaneous views. We could find but one person in town—a somewhat Americanized young fellow named Nik-ke—who was willing to be photographed at all. Another, called Yack—the Zuni stagger at his English nickname—kindly allowed us to photograph the interior of his house, and a most interesting interior it is. But Yack and his female dependents kept religiously out of range of the deadly tube. Children are the most interesting citizens in Zuni—as throughout the world—and we toiled for pictures of

them, but without generally brilliant success. The little rascals were as cognizant of the dangers of the lens as were their elders, and fled like coyotes whenever it was turned their way. We tried focusing in the opposite direction, and then whirling it on them with a snap of the shutter. This worked admirably with a group of recalcitrant old women, but the youngsters were too fleet of foot to be caught in a stern chase even by "30" plates. The only ruse we found successful with them was to focus on a certain point, and abandon the camera, post at the afore-said point a big lump of alleged maple sugar in the hand of the superior seven-eighths of the party—officially known as "Doc"—and then when the young pirates crowded around the dulce, sneak to the camera and pull the trigger. Thus we scored some brilliant victories.

It would also appear from the *Drake's Magazine* article that Lummis engaged in a lively barter session during his time in Zuni. In exchange for sea shells, Lummis secured artifacts of various kinds, primarily stone arrow-points. These he subsequently framed and hung in his home on the Arroyo Seco in Los Angeles. They have since been transferred to the Southwest Museum.

Pueblo Zuni, N.M.   April 1889
This general view of Zuni Pueblo was taken from the southeast. The two poles that appear vertical at the left are part of a ladder that is leaning on the house roof. The angle of Lummis's camera makes the ladder appear to be nearly vertical and without cross-bars. This photograph shows the multistoried architecture of Zuni Pueblo in the nineteenth century and the use of roof entrances to the pueblo's houses. For defensive reasons ground-level doors and windows were rare.

Interior, Pueblo House, Zuni   April 1889
Lummis identifies this Zuni house interior as the home of a man named "Yack" who lived there with "female dependents." As a general rule, this single large room served as kitchen, parlor, bedroom, and workroom. Appended to it was a storage room. In the center rear of the room, one can see a loom with a weaving in progress. The food preparation area to the right is the subject of a detail photograph shot by Lummis. Many of the inhabitants' clothing and bedding was stored over hanging poles such as those seen against the back wall.

Metates (Handmills) in a Zuni House   April 1889
In describing this Zuni room, Lummis noted that at the opposite end of the room from
these grinding stations is the fireplace and cooking area. Here corn is ground on
metates, which are encased in wood or flat stones. Ground corn is moved from station
to station, starting with the most coarse or whole kernels and ending with the finely
ground corn flour or meal. Often several women would grind corn at the same time,
thus making it a communal occasion for women and young girls. Note the brushes,
twined baskets, and painted pottery around the grinding station.

Pueblo Zuni Church   April 1889
The two-story church at Zuni was one of the few structures there in the nineteenth century to be made of adobe. Owing to a scarcity of water, most of the homes were made of stones set in mud mortar and then covered by a mud plaster. The Spanish priests introduced the adobe brick to New Mexico. During Lummis's visit, the few religious items left in the church were guarded by a Zuni named "Mauricio" who assisted Lummis when he copied a Latin passage from a pink silk cloth that hung in the church. Lummis cites this Zuni church as "the most dilapidated" in New Mexico.

92

HOPI PUEBLO

HE HOPI TOWNS of north-central Arizona are located on the southern fringe of the Black Mesa. There, on and about three fingers of the land that jut southward, are a dozen small Hopi towns. Although the terms First, Second, and Third Mesa are used now to identify these land forms, in Lummis's day they were called East, Middle, and West Mesa, respectively. The lack of a permanent water source such as the Rio Grande or its tributaries has conditioned Hopi culture in ways distinct from any of the Pueblos in New Mexico. This is especially true with regard to agricultural practices and religion.

Charles Lummis spent very little time among the Hopi, only three days in August of 1891. His diary shows that on both the twentieth and the twenty-second he was at Keams Canyon, a Hopi and Navajo trading center just to the east of First Mesa; and on the twenty-first he photographed the people and the First Mesa town of Walpi as well as the Snake Dance held there that day.

Lummis used his Hopi photographs soon afterward in April 1892 as the third installment of "Strange Corners of Our Country," then being published as a series of articles in *Harper's Magazine*. There Lummis provides his readers with a credible description of the Snake Dance he witnessed at Walpi the previous year, a dance in which "over one hundred snakes were used." Lummis estimated that sixty-five of these were rattlesnakes.

Lummis found the Snake Dance extremely difficult to photograph. He states that:

There is in existence one photograph which clearly shows the dancers with the snakes—and only one. Beginning so late, and in the deep shadow of the tall houses, it is almost impossible for the dance to be photographed at all; but one year a lucky reflector of white cloud came up and threw a light into the dark corner, and Mr. Wittick got the only perfect picture of the snake-dance.

I have made pictures which do show the snakes; but they are not handsome pictures of the dance. The make-up of the dancers makes photography still harder.

He is referring to Ben Wittick, the photographer from Santa Fe, New Mexico, and to the fact that the dark costume and body paint of the dancers, however striking, does not make for an easy picture.

To fully appreciate the choreography of the Snake Dance as well as its dramatic impact on an audience, one must actually attend the event. Yet Lummis's photography at Walpi and of the Snake Dance captured some of the drama of the architecture and religious ritual. His photos clearly show the Walpi dance plaza as an exquisite stage for ritual drama.

Missing from all of Lummis's writings on the Hopi is the larger view of the Snake Dance in relation to the ritual cycle of the Kachina Cult, the dominant feature of Hopi religion. To see the place of the Snake Dance in the context of Hopi ceremonialism, it must be noted that the Kachina Cult dominates their ritual calendar from December through mid-July, or from the winter solstice beyond the summer solstice. Only after the Kachinas have left the mesas in July do the Women's dances and the Snake Dance occupy the Hopi. Also absent from his diary on the date of this Walpi Snake Dance is any mention of rain, for invariably the Snake Dance brings rain to the mesas. It should be noted that Lummis did not encounter as developed a Kachina Cult with its concern for rain in the pueblos along the Rio Grande, and perhaps this fact left him unfamiliar with the particulars of Hopi religion.

Almost as interesting as the Snake Dancers is the audience at Walpi. When studied carefully, the photographs show that the Snake Dance attracted not only Hopis but also large numbers of Navajos as well as non-Indians. The contrast of Navajo beliefs concerning snakes fascinated Lummis, and he told his readers:

The Navajo Indians have superstitions widely different. . . . They will not touch a snake under any circumstances. So extreme are their prejudices that one of their skilled silver-smiths was beaten nearly to death by his fellows for making

Walpi   August 21, 1891
This untitled photograph shows members of the Snake Society holding snakes in their
mouths and in their hands at an early point in the dance. An overcast sky and/or the
late afternoon hour probably accounts for the dark photograph. The Snake Society's
dance kilt with a white snake design is clearly visible. At the end of the dance, the
snakes are carried to special shrines where they are released, and from there the
snakes begin their journey to the underworld.

me a silver bracelet which represented a rattlesnake, and the obnoxious emblem was promptly destroyed by the raiders— along with the offender's hut.

Within twenty years, the Hopi would prohibit photography at the Snake Dance. The competition among photographers became so rowdy that fist fights between photographers are reported at some Snake Dances in the early part of this century. Although Lummis's images are not perfect, they nevertheless are a valuable record of this unique Hopi ritual.

14 93 — THE MOQUI PUEBLOS — HUALPI. FROM N.E.

Hualpi Dance Court and Kivas   August 21, 1891
This photograph shows the narrow Walpi Plaza perched on the edge of First Mesa
prior to the start of the Snake Dance. The ladder to the left of the photograph is
descending to the Left Over Kiva and the ladder to the right leads to the Two Horned
Kiva. The brush structure to the right of the dance plaza holds the snakes prior to the
dance. Not visible but always present is a foot drum dug in the ground in front of the
brush structure. As the dancers pass the drum, they stamp on it. In his title for this
photograph, Lummis uses an older spelling for Walpi.

Opposite: *Walpi from the N.E.   August 21, 1891*
Lummis indicates that this photograph is from the northeast; however, it is the south
face of the pueblo that is seen. In the foreground below the cliff edge are destroyed
homes and other structures as well as the kachinka, *the resting place used by the*
kachinas between dances in the plaza above.

Walpi   August 21, 1891
A passageway on the south side of Walpi; the stone formation in the center is Snake
Rock. Lummis photographed the Snake Dance in a plaza just in front of this rock.
(Not visible is the stone fetish that was placed in a niche in this rock.)

The Moqui Pueblos—Snake Fetish & Shrine, East Mesa   August 21, 1891
Within this cluster of rocks the spiral stone at the center constitutes the primary
fetish. As such it is thought to possess inherent spiritual power that can be called
upon by individual Hopis. These powers can be activated by placing prayer sticks in
close contact with the fetish. This shrine contains the fetish of the two War Gods.

Pueblo Prayer Sticks   August 21, 1891
Lummis's title is only partially accurate as a label for these miniature objects. The
long stick with feathers wrapped about one end (lower right) is a prayer stick for a
newborn child. The miniature crooks, on the other hand, are paraphernalia of the
Snake Society and represent the wisdom of deceased members of that society. The
miniature strung bows and rings symbolize warfare and hunting powers. All of
these objects would be found at a shrine or an altar.

1400 — A MOQUI MAIDEN — COPYRIGHT 1891 BY C.F. LUMMIS

The Moqui Maiden   August 1891
*Lummis's title correctly defines the marital status of this young woman. Her hair-
style identifies her as unmarried; when she takes a husband, she will no longer wear
her hair in this fashion. The ladder leads to a doorway above.*

SANDIA PUEBLO

LOCATED A DOZEN MILES NORTH of Albuquerque on the east bank of the Rio Grande, Sandia Pueblo is one of two pueblos (the other being Isleta) whose inhabitants speak the southern dialect of Tiwa. These two pueblos, together with Taos and Picuris (the northern Tiwa-speakers) are all that remain of the near twenty Tiwa-speaking pueblos that Coronado encountered in the sixteenth century.

As a result of its proximity to the Rio Grande and to the later city of Albuquerque, Sandia has experienced a great deal of contact with Europeans and Americans. In 1617 it was the seat of the mission of San Francisco, and following the Pueblo Revolt against the Spaniards in 1680, Sandia was abandoned. Many of its inhabitants lived among the Hopi, and in 1681, the pueblo was burned in reprisal by Spaniards. The resettlement of Sandia occurred in the 1740s by former residents, their descendants, as well as by refugees from other pueblos.

The scholarly literature is confusing with regard to the population of Sandia. Prior to the Pueblo Revolt, 3,000 people are estimated to have lived in Sandia, and after resettlement in the 1740s, the pueblo's population was 350. Today the population of Sandia is about 300.

Lummis visited Sandia once, on June 30, 1901. He records in his diary taking six photographs that day, although only five of his glass negatives appear to have survived. His diary entry for that day states:

102

Sandia Pueblo looking east toward the Sandia Mountains. Sandia *means water-melon in the Spanish language, but its native language name is* Nafeat, *meaning dusty or sandy place.   September 11, 1901*

Salimos todos en carriage para Sandia. Foto alli 6 veces, iglesia primera, plaza, pueblo con Sandians. De regresa, Bob, Dick, T y yo.

In translation this would read approximately as follows:

We left for Sandia in a carriage. Took 6 photographs there, of church, plaza, pueblo with Indians. Upon return it was Bob, Dick, T and I.

The effort of travel by horse-drawn carriage can only be imagined here, but in other accounts, Lummis was agonizingly graphic in his description of road and travel conditions to many of the pueblos.

An unidentified location at Sandia in 1901. In the foreground are gardens. The adobe walls and the oven seen in the background are both the result of Spanish settlement in New Mexico.

SANTA ANA

SANTA ANA sits on the north bank of the Jemez River, above Albuquerque and to the west of the Rio Grande. Its inhabitants speak the eastern dialect of Keresan. In Lummis's day, its population numbered approximately two hundred. Today most of its former residents and their descendants live in and about Bernalillo, New Mexico, and return to the pueblo only for important ritual occasions. The most significant fiesta occurs on July 26, the feast of St. Anne.

On September 16, 1901, Lummis made six photographs of Santa Ana Pueblo. In his diary for that date he stated:

Ruins 200 yards en cuadrado, 3 sides, 4th on river, was 6 & 7 stories high. Hallo 2 puntas y hachita finisima. Llegamos Santa Ana, caamino jurnamente arendso 3:30. Photos y trato trinajas. Photo pueblo, church, estufa, plaza & c. Salimos 4:30 mas a prisma. At head of grade photo Sandia mountains & valley. Llegamos Bernalillo at 7:00.

As a loose translation some of this Spanish would read:

After an arduous trek we arrived at Santa Ana at 3:30. Took photos . . . of pueblo, church, kiva, plaza, etc. We left at 4:30 traveling much faster. At head of grade photo of Sandia Mountains and valley. We arrived at Bernalillo at 7:00.

Turquoise Kiva, Santa Ana Pueblo. This is one of two kivas at Santa Ana to which every member of the pueblo belongs. The other, Pumpkin (or Squash) Kiva, is located nearby, and individuals associate with one or the other on the basis of clan affiliation. One's kiva group serves to direct the pueblo's medicine societies as well as various rituals held throughout the year.

JEMEZ AND PECOS PUEBLOS

THE VILLAGE OF JEMEZ, located on the east bank of the Jemez River, represents a series of removals and relocations of Towa-speaking peoples from other village sites both near and far from its present day location. At the time of first contact in the sixteenth century, the population estimates for Jemez range from three thousand to five thousand. It is difficult to tell from early Spanish sources just which villages are included in this figure, for in fact there were at this time many Towa-speaking pueblos along the Jemez River and its tributaries. Poor soil available to aboriginal farmers necessitated a relatively dispersed settlement pattern in the Jemez Valley. Beyond this Jemez region, the Spanish explorers of New Mexico also encountered numerous Towa-speaking pueblos far to the east near Pecos. The last relocation to Jemez occurred in 1838 when the twenty or so Towa-speaking survivors of Pecos Pueblo abandoned it and moved to Jemez.

When Lummis visited Jemez in 1912, its population was slightly more than five hundred, and one could estimate that approximately twenty percent of these residents were descendants of Pecos refugees. In October of that year, he arrived at Jemez with his son, Quimo. Their visit also included side trips to nearby archaeological ruins, and his diary shows that only on October 7 and 8 and again from the sixteenth through the nineteenth was he actually in Jemez. The rest of the time he and Quimo spent in the surrounding area. During the latter stay, Quimo was ill and Lummis took no photographs, and from the earlier visit, no photographs taken from within the pueblo exist.

The best known of the Towa-speaking refugees to have settled in Jemez were the inhabitants of Pecos Pueblo, located about twenty miles southeast of Santa Fe in a valley formed by the Pecos River. The people of Pecos spoke a dialect of Towa, a branch of the Kiowa-Tanowa language family that was also spoken at Jemez Pueblo. Although prehistoric Pueblo settlements in the Pecos Valley began in the 1100s, the existing Pecos site was not occupied until the 1300s, and because of its eastern location, Pecos was an important center for trade between the Plains and the Rio Grande Pueblos.

In 1540, Pecos received members of Coronado's expedition, and by the year 1600, the pueblo was being used as a staging center for Spanish missionary activities in the Pecos Valley as well as to the east on the Plains. It was this proximity to the Plains, however, that forced Pecos to seek allies, first with Apaches and later with Spaniards, to ward off the attacks by Comanches. From resident Spaniards, the people of Pecos learned numerous Spanish crafts that they practiced both at the pueblo and later in the small Spanish towns that formed in the Pecos Valley.

In addition to the attacks from Plains Indians, the people of Pecos suffered greatly from European diseases, especially smallpox. By the start of the nineteenth century, what had been a pueblo of two thousand people was reduced to one of less than two hundred. In 1838, Pecos was abandoned, and its few inhabitants took refuge with relatives in the nearby Spanish towns and in the pueblo of Jemez.

These two photographs are opposite views of the pueblo of Giusewa near Jemez Springs (1912). In the photograph on the right the recent historic buildings are visible in the upper left, while in the photograph on the left, the church and house walls can be seen. Giusewa was abandoned in the 1630s.

JEMEZ, GIUSEWA
LUMMIS – OCT. 7, 1912

Distant view of the seventeenth-century Spanish church at Pecos   1890

Interior of the Pecos church   1890

113

SAN FELIPE PUEBLO

ON SEPTEMBER 21, 1901, Lummis visited the Keresan pueblo of San Felipe and secured eight photographs. In his diary for that date he states:

> . . . went across the river over the bridge of the Indians. I climbed the mesa and took photos of the bridge, the Rio Grande and the ruins of old San Felipe; I then climbed down and took pictures of the bridge and the Mesa Redonda. We went to the pueblo and socialized. We returned quickly, in 1½ hours, arriving at Bernalillo at 6:25. I found an ancient spur at San Felipe. . . .

In addition to several distant and close-up views of the ruins of the old pueblo, Lummis made three shots of the early bridge across the Rio Grande. In years past, the bridge's importance resulted from the pueblo's historic location on either side of the Rio Grande. That in essence is what Coronado saw in 1540: two thriving pueblos of three and four storied houses on either side of the river. Today only the west side pueblo exists, and its population of almost two thousand is probably twice as large as the two pueblos of earlier times.

Lummis published a San Felipe folk tale in an undated newspaper article and again in 1891 in *A New Mexico David*, a collection of his previously published stories. It involved the continuing conflict between the Pueblos and the Spaniards in the late seventeenth century. The tale that Lummis published was the story of Fray Alonzo Ximenes de Cisneros, a Spanish priest stationed at Cochiti.

114

Charles F. Lummis's shadow in his photograph of the bridge over the Rio Grande at San Felipe   September 21, 1901

According to Lummis's informant, Teodosio Duran, a former governor of San Felipe, the people of Cochiti were plotting to kill the resident priest when he was warned by his Indian assistant, the sacristan. The priest escaped to San Felipe, but his discovery there caused the Cochiti to lay siege to San Felipe. Their siege was broken by means of a miracle that caused water instead of blood to flow from wounds inflicted on the priest's arm.

San Felipe from the East   September 1901
This title is listed in Lummis's scrapbook.

116

SANTO DOMINGO PUEBLO

S ANTO DOMINGO PUEBLO is located about forty miles north of Albuquerque, on the east side of the Rio Grande and to the south of the Galisteo Arroyo. In the eighteenth century, the pueblo was organized about a central plaza, but since the mid-nineteenth century, its houses have been arranged in parallel rows running east to west toward the Rio Grande. Some of these homes are two-storied, and at the western edge of the pueblo the row-housing pattern becomes less regular. The eastern boundary of the pueblo's housing area is an irrigation ditch that brings water from the Rio Grande to the pueblo's fields. Beyond this ditch are the Roman Catholic church, a cemetery, and a recently constructed community center.

The language of Santo Domingo is Keresan, which linguists divide into two dialects, Eastern and Western. Sharing the Eastern Keresan dialect with the people of Santo Domingo are the Puebloans at Cochiti, San Felipe, Santa Ana, and Zia. Western Keresan is spoken at Acoma and Laguna.

For at least the last one hundred years, Santo Domingo has supported a large population by Pueblo standards. In 1807, its population is estimated to have been about one thousand and in 1888 when Lummis first visited the pueblo, the population was just slightly larger. However, by 1970, it had a total of twenty-three hundred people, living in almost five hundred households.

Throughout the nineteenth and the twentieth centuries, this population has been considered to be among the most conservative of the Rio Grande Pueblos. The reticence of the residents of Santo Domingo to divulge their lifeways is legendary as is their wariness of outsiders. But on at least one day each year—the "Saint's Day"—their hospitality is just as famous.

August 4 marks the major feast day at Santo Domingo Pueblo. Within the Roman Catholic liturgical calendar, the feast of St. Dominic is celebrated, and at Santo Domingo the so-called Corn, or Tablita, Dance is held on this feast day of the pueblo's patron saint. In 1979, the anthropologist Charles Lange described the Corn Dance and its importance as follows:

> In size, careful costuming, and in conscientiously executed performance, this is a genuinely spectacular event that has long been an attraction to the Santo Domingo Indians, residents and absentees, Indians from neighboring villages, and non-Indians as well.

And writing in 1894, the U.S. government's Indian agent, H. R. Poorer, states that this dance is regarded among "the finest to be seen among the pueblos."

Lummis came twice to see the Corn Dance at Santo Domingo, in 1888 and again in 1891. On the first occasion, he was accompanied by Adolph Bandelier, the Swiss ethnologist. They traveled there on the Atchison, Topeka and Santa Fe Railway, debarking at the tiny stop of Wallace, New Mexico (later known as Domingo Station) near the eastern side of the pueblo.

After his visit in 1888, Lummis wrote the article "Feast and Dance Among the Pueblos of Santo Domingo." The article appeared in the *Boston Globe* on May 12, 1889, and some of the photographs Lummis took in 1888 were reproduced as line drawing illustrations by the *Boston Globe*. There seems to be no evidence to suggest that Lummis photographed the Corn Dance of 1891, although he did photograph architectural features as well as the governor of Cochiti, Jose Hilario Montoya, who was a spectator at the dance that year. From his diary entry for August 4, 1891, we learn that he was prohibited from photographing the dance and the kiva. Thus, in the intervening two years from 1888 to 1891, the Pueblo had determined that photography, or at least Lummis's picture-taking of the dance and the kiva, would be restricted. However, it should be noted that on both occasions, Lummis was accompanied by Adolph Bandelier, and the Pueblos' attitude toward the Swiss scholar may have colored their view of Lummis.

Lummis visited Frijoles Canyon just to the north and west of Santo Domingo on five different occasions (1890, 1891, 1912, 1913, and 1927) usually in the month of August. Both the Cochiti as well as the Santo Domingo people believe that the Frijoles Canyon area constitutes the ancestral home of their pueblos. It was here that Lummis photographed a variety of prehistoric and early historic house and kiva ruins.

The Corn Dance photographs of 1888 are some of Lummis's most significant views of Pueblo ceremonials, and his article of 1889 discusses the audience, the difficulties he encountered in photographing at Santo Domingo, and the dance itself, in just about this order of importance.

First the spectators:

All day Friday heterogeneous and disjointed caravans were leaking into Santo Domingo by four roads. Down the fearful Labajarda hill bumped a couple of Uncle Sam's roomy ambulances freighted with beaux and belles from Santa Fe. From Wallace thundered big farm wagons, heavy with "the boys" from the mines of Golden, San Pedro and Cerillos. Along the river road trundled other wagons with Pueblo families from Cochiti or Mexicans from Pena Blanca. Similar processions straggled up from the Pueblo of San Felipe, whose remarkable old church crowns a mesa promontory six miles down stream. And across the swift current came splashing mounted Navajoes from their reservation 100 miles to the west to join the festivities, sell their matchless blankets and their tireless ponies and snap up such unconsidered trifles as might fall in their way.

Concerning his difficulty in securing photographs he stated:

The camera and I had taken up a claim at the side front of the booth, so as to sweep the plaza; but now my venerable aboriginal friend, Ignacio Chama, governor of Santo Domingo, swooped down on us like a house afire. I was giving my three hundredth Pueblo a peep through the magic glass when Ignacio planted himself squarely in front, his feet a yard apart, and with much bowing, waving of hands and pulmonary explosion, gave us one of the ablest stump speeches that has been heard in Santo Domingo for many a day. He's a natural politician as El Gubernador, and never lets a chance get away to make capital for himself. He expatiated in very good Spanish on the magnitude of feast, the ability of the dancers and the

amount of real estate they would require for their manoeu-
vres and wound up by remarking that we would have to move,
and that quickly.

"Pero, amigo," I began with that fine Italian diplomacy
which is so essential to him who seeks photographic favors in
this un-amateured territory; but he cut me off short, and
informed me that he was running this affair and that until I
got elected governor I'd better mind him. Then the pompous
but kind-hearted old man strutted off, only to hunt me up
later in a quiet corner, saying he was sorry, but he had to
maintain his authority, and—would I give him the ingredients
of a cigarette?

And his description of the dance:

Meanwhile 80 dancers, two abreast, came dilly-dallying up
until the foremost were at the booth, and then the long line
whose couples were of alternate sex doubled upon itself and
dilly-dallied back to the middle of the plaza, each dancer bend-
ing to the plaster saint as he or she passed it. The dance,
though on a Catholic saint's day and under Catholic auspices,
had no other tang of Rome about it, but was one of the many
mystic rites of the never-forgotten sun worship of the Pueblos. They have many different dances, known as the sun
dance, the turtle dance, the harvest dance, etc., but all out-
wardly so much alike that the stranger is not apt to find any
difference between them. The dresses and the figures are
almost identical. This was the green corn dance, though the
average visitor wouldn't know the fact without a label.

The male dancers were stripped to the waist, and wore
only their moccasins, leggings and a unique dancing skirt
which fell half way to the knee, and was adorned with a
curious cord sash at the side and an exquisite fox skin behind.
Each held in one hand a sprig of evergreen, and in the other a
gourd rattle painted black with which he emphasized the
rhythm of the music to which he danced, the chanting of the
chorus and the grunting of the tombe. The women wore their
usual dress with the exception of the dainty moccasins, the fat
buckskin boots and the reboso (head shawl), all of which were
omitted. They held an evergreen branch in each hand, and
with them kept gentle time. They wore upon their heads
curious affairs sawed from boards.

So, filing up and down the plaza in couples, or wheeling

120

into long parallel ranks which countermarched and inter-marched, the sing-song music and the hip-hop dance kept up for seven hours. When the first relay of 80 dancers had spread themselves thus for half an hour they danced slowly out a side street and back to the estufa, while relay No. 2, of equal numbers danced with equal deliberateness into the plaza from the opposite end.

Lummis was not unaware of Santo Domingo social organization and its interrelationships with religious ritual. Also, Lummis often uses the Spanish term *estufa* meaning "hot room" as a substitute for kiva, and in this *Boston Globe* article he discusses the various numbers of kivas in different pueblos. However, in this newspaper article for a general readership, he avoids any lengthy discourse on the kiva group's role in Pueblo life. Here he does note their place in the choreography of the dance in terms of the advance and retreat patterns that juxtapose the Turquoise and Squash kivas. Undoubt-edly, the published work of the Indian Agent H. R. Poorer and that of the army officer Captain John G. Bourke, both Lummis's contemporaries, are more detailed in their concern for the social context of the religious rituals. Yet their writings are unlikely to have been read by a general audience in the late nineteenth century.

Following pages: *Corn Dance   1888*

Copyright 1886
C.F. Lummis

COCHITI PUEBLO

COCHITI PUEBLO, located thirty miles south of Santa Fe, New Mexico, on the west side of the Rio Grande, shares with the residents of Santo Domingo and San Felipe the eastern dialect of the Keresan language. It figures large in Lummis's pueblo travels because of his early friendship with Adolph Bandelier, the Swiss ethnographer-archaeologist, who lived for extended periods at Cochiti.

On July 14, 1888, Lummis spent the day at Cochiti with Bandelier, his early mentor in the Southwest. Undoubtedly, July 14 was chosen as the date for their visit because it marks the feast day of San Buenaventura, the patron saint of Cochiti's Catholic mission church, and the festivities at the pueblo on this day are among the most important of the year.

The popular term used to describe the dance that Lummis photographed on this date is the "Corn Dance." This is the term Lummis employed; however, the term preferred by the Cochiti is that of the "Tablita Dance." The dance is so named because of the high, flat headgear or crown worn by the women while dancing.

Another Lummis visit to Cochiti occurred over a seven-day period in 1890, from October 9–16. During this visit he again accompanied Bandelier but not for the purpose of photographing ceremonial activity in the pueblo. Instead, the purpose of their trip was to photograph the so-called stone lions of Cochiti and the prehistoric archaeological sites in the Rito de los Frijoles area. No more than ten Lummis photographs exist of Cochiti Pueblo itself from the 1888 visit, yet for its nearby archaeological sites of the Rito de los Frijoles, Lummis made dozens of views and returned again in August of 1910, 1911, 1912, and 1913 to photograph them.

Lummis recounts witnessing the Cochiti Corn Dance in *The Land of Poco Tiempo* (1893). Yet he first published the description as a newspaper article on July 29, 1888 in the Boston *Globe-Democrat* entitled "A Sun Dance at Cochiti, How a Pueblo Town Celebrates the Feast of its Patron Saint." In addition to the distinctive headgear worn by the women dancers, two highly decorated poles are carried by each of the two groups of dancers. The organization and the sequence of the dance, as well as the costuming of the dancers and the antics of the Koshare clowns who accompany the dancers, are discussed by Lummis. Clearly the choreography of the dancing was very impressive to Lummis. Concerning the harmony of the dancers he states:

> The soft pat of the moccasined feet of the men and the bare soles of the women was audible only in the aggregate.

It is difficult to know the depth of Lummis's knowledge of Pueblo culture in general and Cochiti culture in particular at the time of his July visit in 1888 and the subsequent article. He perceived that there were two groups dancing and their costumes differed at least in the detail of the women's headgear. That Lummis understood the groups differed in terms of their kiva affiliations, Pumpkin and Turquoise, we do not know; however, armed with other information, a close examination of the *tablitas* allows us to identify which kiva group is pictured. Lummis, for example, states:

> The only difference between this ballet and the first was that the women's headdresses in this were arched at the top while in the first they were serrate.

The archaeology of Cochiti fascinated Lummis, and he wrote about it in several publications. In one, "The Wanderings of Cochiti," he traced the movement of Keresan speakers from earlier site locations where archaeologists had excavated. He employed Cochiti folklore to supplement the archaeology. One of his favorite Cochiti informants was Jose Hilario Montoya, whom he cited in the above article as being observed in the Rito de los Frijoles area:

> In a cave room of the cluster which has suffered most from the erosion of the cliff, I once stumbled upon gentle Jose Hilario Montoya . . . wrapped in his blanket and in reverie. He had stolen away from us, to dream an hour in the specific house that was of his own first grandfathers.

In the history of American anthropology, Lummis was an early student concerned with the validation of archaeology by oral traditions.

125

WATCHING THE DANCE,
PUEBLO OF COCHITI.

The date of origin of these "stone lions" is unknown; however, because of their association with prehistoric ruins, it is generally assumed that they pre-date the arrival of the Spaniards. It is known that in historic times, Cochiti hunters would pass by them and place offerings of red ochre in the eyes of the lions as a means of assuring success in their hunting. The association of an offering with eyesight is generally thought to ensure keen eyesight for the hunter.

Preceding pages: *Watching the Dance   July 14, 1888*

View of the Cochiti Tablita Dance of July 14, 1888. The dance is referred to as both a "Tablita Dance" and as a "Corn Dance." The flat board above the women's head is the tablita. *The design style seen here is that of the Turquoise Kiva's members. If the* tablita *had but three stepped points and no carved half-moon, it would designate the Pumpkin Kiva. The tall decorated pole differs between the two kivas.*

SAN ILDEFONSO PUEBLO

THE HISTORY OF San Ildefonso during Lummis's lifetime in the late nineteenth and early twentieth centuries is a complex one. It marks a period of great stress within the pueblo as well as one of dramatic change in the non-Indian world surrounding the village. In cultural pattern, San Ildefonso was similar to its Tewa-speaking neighbor, Santa Clara Pueblo; however, in the 1880s, the people of San Ildefonso realigned their village to the north of its former location. This removal to the north changed the relative position of the kivas and the dance plazas within the pueblo and caused such severe disagreements between families that the traditional patterns of social and ritual organization were disrupted. It would appear that Lummis was either unaware of or disinterested in this social situation, for there is no mention of it in his writings.

Lummis was in San Ildefonso the first time on July 28, 1889. Only two photographs of the thirteen taken during this visit have survived, and in both photographs the pueblo's Catholic religious structures, church, and *convento* are the subjects. His diary mentions a dance on that date; however, he did not or was not allowed to photograph it. His second and last visit to San Ildefonso occurred in November 1926, and no photographs exist that were taken on that trip. Lummis did photograph a San Ildefonso resident, Juan Gonzales, but that photograph was taken a few days earlier in Santa Fe, New Mexico.

130

Old Church, Pueblo of San Ildefonso
Lummis photographed this church in 1889, fifteen years before it was razed.
Historically San Ildefonso's church shared its priest with the church at Santa Clara
Pueblo and at various times each was serviced by a priest residing in the other pueblo.

Juan Gonzales, San Ildefonso Pueblo (right) Manuel Vargas, Picuris Pueblo
(left)   November 17, 1926
This photograph was taken in Santa Fe at a meeting of the Pueblo Council.

The Governor's All-Pueblo Council   1926

SANTA CLARA PUEBLO

SANTA CLARA PUEBLO, along with San Juan and San Ildefonso, constitute three of the group of six linguistically related villages that are identified as the northern Tewa-speaking pueblos. As with many of the pueblos, they are identified by the Spanish-derived name of the patron saint of the church located there. St. Clare lived in the thirteenth century as a contemporary of St. Francis of Assisi and founded a congregation of nuns, the Second Franciscan Order, also called the "Poor Clares." She died in 1253 and her memory was brought to New Mexico by the Spanish missionaries of the sixteenth century. The other three northern Tewa-speaking pueblos—Nambe, Pojoaque, and Tesuque—have all retained their Tewa names.

The pueblo of Santa Clara had suffered greatly since the arrival of the Spaniards. It is estimated that over five hundred people died in 1782 from a smallpox epidemic at Santa Clara and San Juan. In 1889, at the time of Lummis's first visit, the population was probably fewer than three hundred, and by 1929, there were only four hundred people in residence. By 1970, the pueblo's population was approximately fifteen hundred.

On August 12, 1889, the feast day of St. Clare, Lummis photographed the dance that occurs annually on this date. On September 17, 1926, Lummis again visited Santa Clara Pueblo. At this time he viewed the Rainbow and Eagle dances, but he did not or was not allowed to photograph them. Instead he took four photographs of Santiago Naranjo, a Pueblo leader.

Lummis's last visit to Santa Clara occurred in 1927. His diary description for August 12 of that year gives both the facts and the flavor of that visit:

Leave Santa Fe at 10:25 with Paul Reiter & Miss Eleanor Johnson. We strike out old Tesuque Road in fine shape; through Tesuque, Pojoaque, Bouquet Ranch, Espanola to Santa Clara. There find Dr. Clyde Fisher at work with movie camera—he makes movies of us with Santiago, Tony Lujan; Juan Concha Grande y otros de Taos. Mrs. Fisher, young Reed (F's assistant) & 20 on Sanatiago me abraza. Lo doy en Dechel. Much pleased. Tony y dermas Taos crowd glad to see me. Gov. of Santa Clara, Juan Jose Gutierrez very nice. Many from San Juan and Cochiti; but see none from Jemez or Isleta. Big crowd—Mexican & American—over 500 . . . was difficult to see because of the big crowd.

He also mentions that he took seven Kodak pictures when the dancers danced past the "W estufa" (meaning the west kiva). These photographs are unlocated.

The Pueblo dancers in the center of this photograph are almost lost in the crowd of non-Indian spectators. The horse-drawn transport is in sharp contrast to the scene that confronted Lummis when he returned to Santa Clara in 1926 and 1927. Then he traveled by car and visited two other pueblos the same day.

Santiago Naranjo

PUYÉ

THE PREHISTORIC SITE of Puyé on the Pajarito Plateau is one of the most extensive "Cliff Cities" of the Southwest. It is located in the Rio Grande Valley about thirty miles north of Santa Fe and ten miles west of Espanola on the west side of the Rio Grande near Santa Clara Pueblo. Although references to its existence appear as early as 1880, systematic excavation did not begin until the summer of 1907. That work, directed by Edgar L. Hewett, was sponsored by the Southwest Society, the Los Angeles based chapter of the Archaeological Institute of America.

The Southwest Society of the Archaeological Institute of America was founded, of course, by Charles F. Lummis, and his prefatory words to Hewett's 1909 article in *Out West* leave no doubt as to his association with the site. The Southwest Society would later become the Southwest Museum in Los Angeles.

The work described by Dr. Hewett has left a monument comparable to the work of governments and scientific bodies in Italy, Greece, Palestine, Mexico, Egypt, etc. This noble American ruin is already visited by hundreds of tourists. The wonderfully interesting antiquities from it now rest in the Southwest Museum rooms in Los Angeles.

It is admitted that the development of American archaeology in the Institute dates from the organization of the Southwest Society. It is also admitted that no other archaeological society in the United States has accomplished as much in active work for its own community as well as for the world of science.

Quite apart from Lummis's expansive statement above, it should be noted that Puyé, now administered by the Santa Clara Tribe, was one of the earliest sites in the Southwest to be excavated by professional archaeologists. Its relatively close proximity to Santa Fe also caused it to be an important attraction to early tourists in New Mexico. Lummis visited Puyé on two occasions, once in 1890 and again in 1909. On both trips he photographed the ruins, and today twenty-three views have survived.

In a sense Puyé is two sites. One, atop the Puyé Mesa, is a pueblo consisting of more than one thousand rooms, constructed of tufa—a lightweight, porous, volcanic stone that the pueblo's prehistoric residents shaped into blocks for their walls. The second site, running for more than a mile along the base of the mesa, consists of two levels of cave dwellings that had stone rooms extending out from the caves. In addition to the mesa-top rooms and the caves along the mesa's talus slope, the Puyé site has ten kivas and a prehistoric reservoir near the mesa-top pueblo.

Puyé was occupied from the thirteenth to the sixteenth century, and its residents may have been the ancestors to the modern-day Puebloans at Santa Clara. Today, as in Lummis's time, Puyé is located on Santa Clara Pueblo land, and each year, in late July, the Santa Clara Indians conduct annual festivities there.

The excavation of a kiva at Puyé atop the Pajarito Plateau. In the background are the weathered houses of the prehistoric settlement, and in the foreground is an excavated kiva. A total of ten kivas were excavated at Puyé.

Opposite: *Cave Dwellings at Puyé Santa Clara Cañon, N.M.   1890*
The holes in the cliff face above the caves supported roof poles that extended out from the cliff to provide for one or more rooms in front of the cave.

An excavation in progress at Puyé in the summer of 1909. This research was sponsored in part by the Southwest Society, the Los Angeles Chapter of the Archaeological Institute of America.

142

TAOS PUEBLO

OCATED SEVENTY MILES NORTH of Santa Fe, Taos is today
the most northern of the Pueblo communities in New Mexico. In
Lummis's "tramp across the continent" in 1884-85, he did not
visit Taos. Instead he stayed close to the Rio Grande as he came south
from Colorado. At that time the pueblo was much more isolated than
it is today and had yet to be "discovered" by artists or tourists. In an
article for the *Los Angeles Times* written on October 30, 1889, Lummis
stated:

> There are many bad roads in New Mexico and many ugly
> journeys; but I do not now remember any that for straight-
> out 40 mile meanness quite equals the way to Taos.

He was referring here to the mountain road from Santa Fe to Taos.

Lummis visited Taos Pueblo on two widely separated occasions.
His first visit was from September 29 to October 1, 1889, when he
attended the festivities that surround the feast of St. Geronimo. His
second visit came two years before his death, on August 16 and 17,
1926.

The pueblo changed significantly between the time of his two
visits, expanding from a community of 400 to one of more than 650.
However, more importantly, the vast majority of the people of Taos
that Lummis first encountered lived in North and South Houses, the
four and five level apartment houses within the walled compound of
the pueblo. By 1926, many families had abandoned their traditional
homes, establishing single-family households on the common lands
that surround the pueblo.

During his first stay at Taos, Lummis took thirty-five photos. He traveled to the pueblo in order to observe the community celebrating one of its major feast days, St. Geronimo's Day (September 30). At this time Lummis photographed both North House and South House, the running races that pit kiva societies against each other, and the pole climbing event by the "Black Eyes," also known as the Koshare Clowns.

In his October 1889 *Times* article, he referred to the two multi-storied housing complexes of Taos as "two wonderful human bee-hives." And in the open space between the two complexes, he stated, "were drawn up a thousand huddled vehicles of every description." One week later, on November 6, again in the *Los Angeles Times*, he described the activities he saw and some which he could only imagine:

> When a Pueblo feast day draws near there are other things to be done besides the baking of festal bread and cakes. . . . In the dark, close estufas (secret and sacred council chambers) there are remarkable preliminary 'goings-on' for days and weeks.

Lummis's concern and curiosity for the activities of the kivas is understandable, for it is from one of the kivas at North House that the thirty or more near-nude men emerged for the dances and races that characterize much of the public ritual of San Geronimo's Day.

Lummis notes in this second article that one of the leaders of the kiva groups objected to the presence of his camera near the race course:

> I had just snapped the shutter on the one plate and was preparing for another, when the captain walked up to me, put up his hand in front of the tube and said very courteously and in a remarkably sonorous voice: "No *amigo*. Anything else, but the *principales* do not wish any pictures made of the races." All this in Spanish, of course, I used to argue with these fellows, but know better now; and the camera went back in the case, and the case to the house, while I took a mean advantage—and several pictures—with a Kodak, to the knowledge of whose subterfuges my aboriginal friend had not yet graduated.

Only one Kodak camera photograph, seen here with Lummis's title, "Pueblo of Taos, N.M., Foot-Race," survives.

The public festivities on San Geronimo's Day ended in the late afternoon when the dancers again emerged from the kiva and proceeded to the courtyard in front of the church. There a fifty foot

144

peeled pine pole with a cross-bar had been erected. Hanging tied to it were "a fat sheep, a sack of feast bread, several yards of calico and other prizes," and the dancers scaled the pole to retrieve these offerings.

In 1927, Lummis was much more concerned with making portraits of various individuals that he encountered at the pueblo, both Indian and non-Indian. These include such persons as Juan Concha Grande, Manuel Mandrason, Jerry Mirabel, Alberto and Juanito Lujan, and Jose and Juan Concha. In addition to these portraits he also photographed Kit Carson's grave, a street scene in the city of Taos, a Dr. T. P. Martin, and the plaza at Rancho de Taos.

This 1927 trip by automobile to the pueblos was for Lummis a "last hurrah." He never returned to New Mexico, and he would die in one year of cancer. Yet even on his death bed, he was working with a daughter to edit his journals and writings that described his life-long love affair with the Southwest.

This view of South House also shows a field of squash and/or pumpkin and the wall that separated the pueblo from the field, built to protect the people of Taos from marauding bands of Plains Indians. The wooden racks seen on either side of the wall are used for drying and storing animal fodder.

146

The structure seen here behind the animal corrals is all that remained in Lummis's time of the first Catholic church in Taos. This church was built in 1728 and destroyed in 1847 by American forces sent from Santa Fe to end a rebellion against the United States. To pierce the church's three-foot-thick adobe walls, the American commander bombarded the church with artillery and then stormed it with troops. Lummis used this image in his book A New Mexico David *without any mention of the story about it.*

Taos Pueblo Distant View. South House is to the left.

Jose de la Cruz Concha and Juan Ysidro Concha of Taos Pueblo   November 5, 1926

Opposite: *The painter Albert Lujan of Taos Pueblo. The shadow in the lower right is Charles Lummis's.   November 4, 1926*

150

The wall in the foreground of this photograph is that of the new church of St. Geronimo, built after 1850. Just to the right of the doorway is the pole used by the Black Eyes (the clown society) during the festivities surrounding the feast of San Geronimo.

This footrace was photographed by Lummis in 1889. At Taos, such races pit kiva groups against one another, and yet the symbolism of the races moves far beyond the human participants, transforming the races into ritual acts by the runners.